NICHOLAS MAW

Sonata Notturna

(1985)

for cello and string orchestra

FABER MUSIC

Sonata Notturna was commissioned by the 1985 King's Lynn Festival
with funds provided by the Arts Council of Great Britain
and first performed by Alexander Baillie and the
Peterborough String Orchestra in the Fermoy Centre,
King's Lynn on 30 May 1986

Duration: c. 25 minutes

Minimum string strength: 12 players (4.3.2.2.1)

(444/89)   Hobbs the Printers of Southampton

SONATA NOTTURNA

I INTRADA

Tempo molto sostenuto, poco rubato
(♩ = c. 52)

NICHOLAS MAW

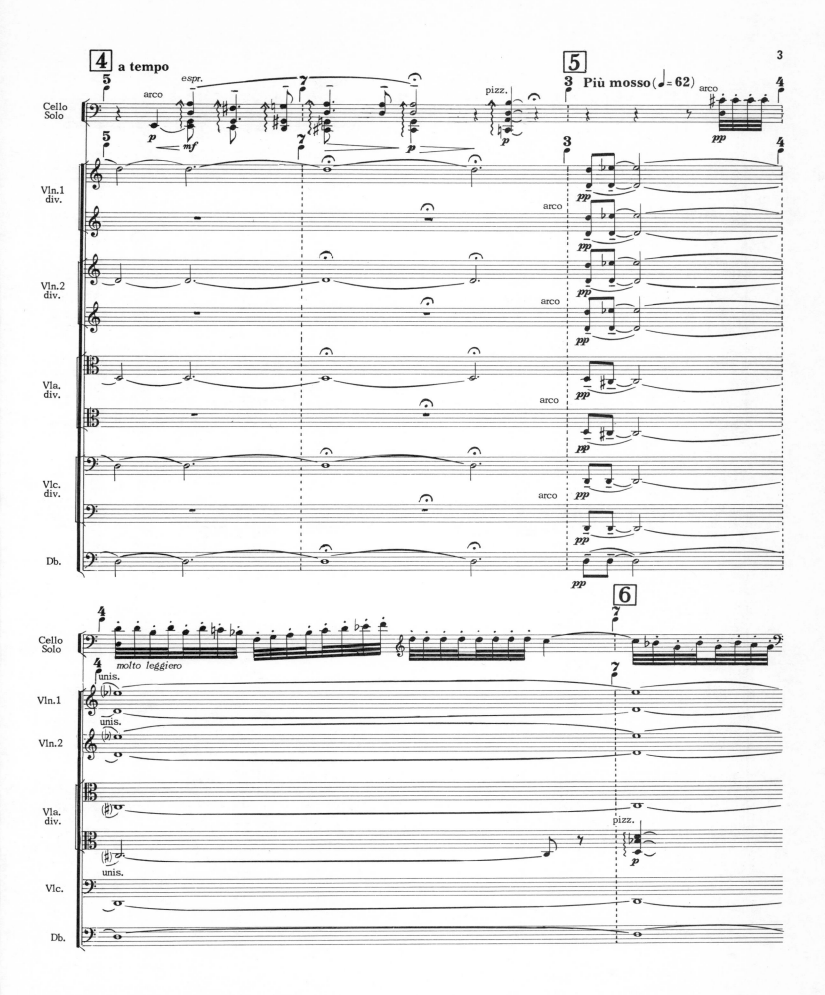

4

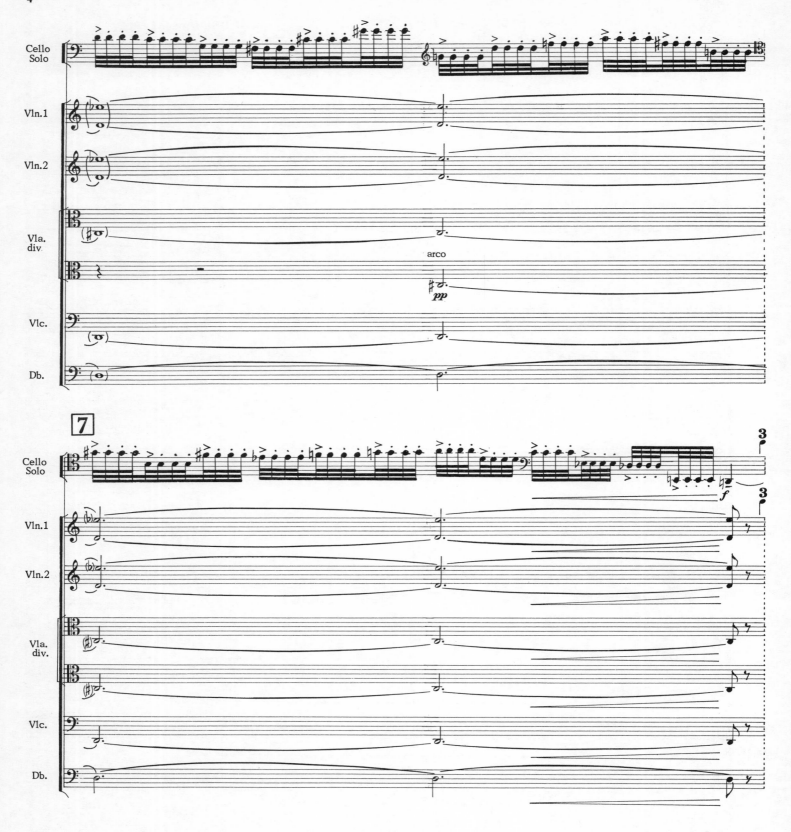

II CANTO

III CADENZA

IV CAPRICCIO

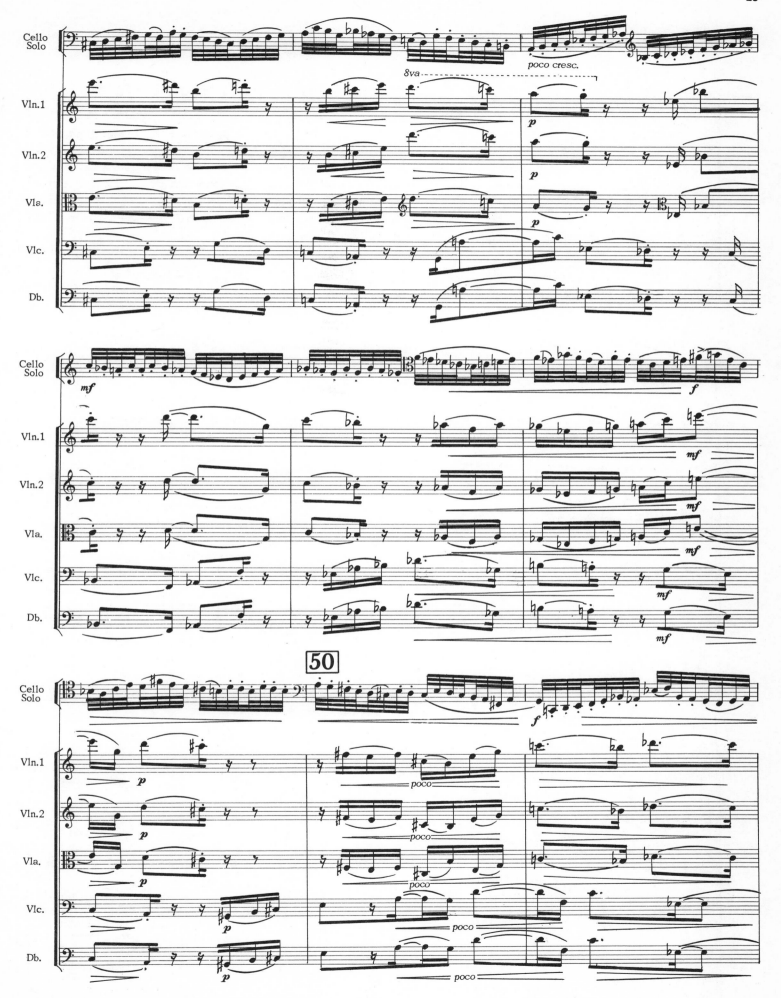

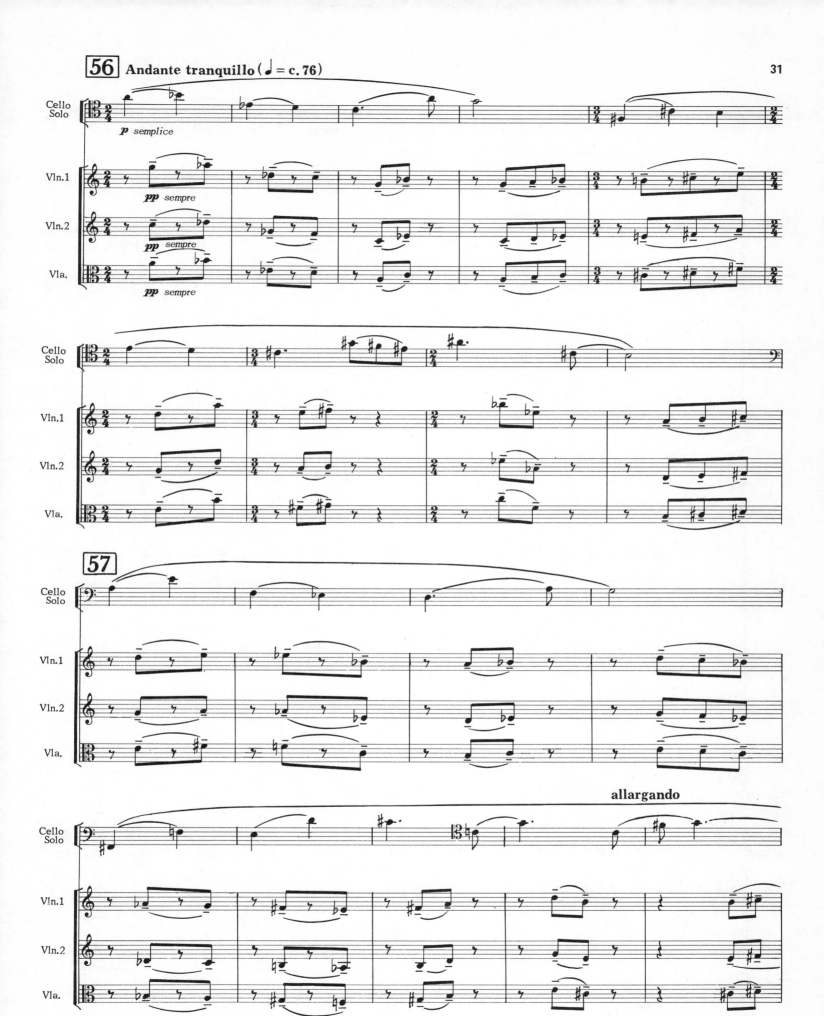

64 (l'istesso tempo)

L'istesso tempo, ma
senza rigore

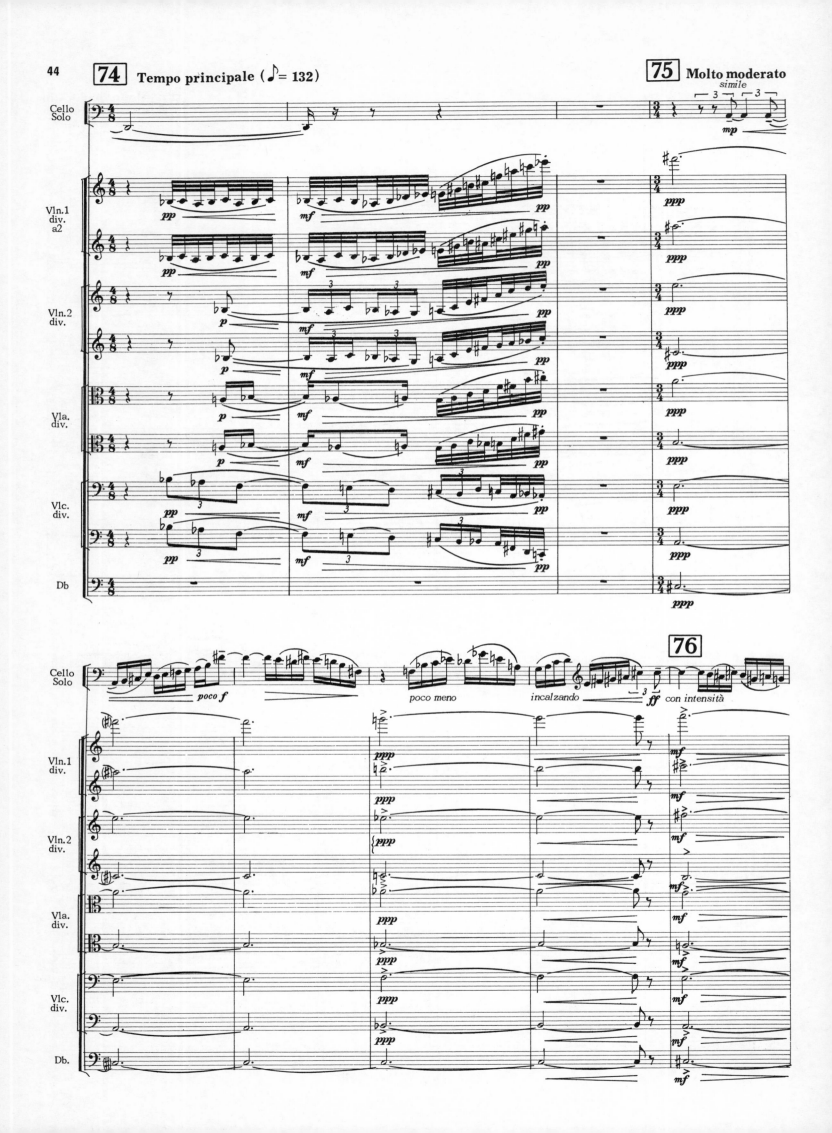

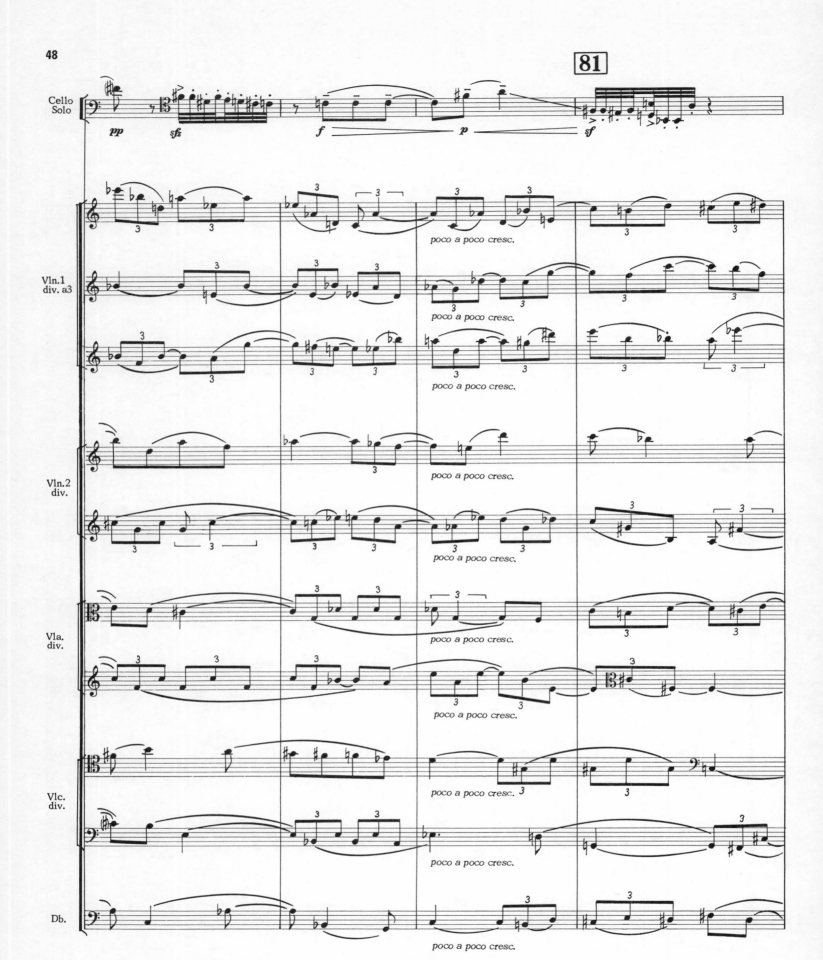

49

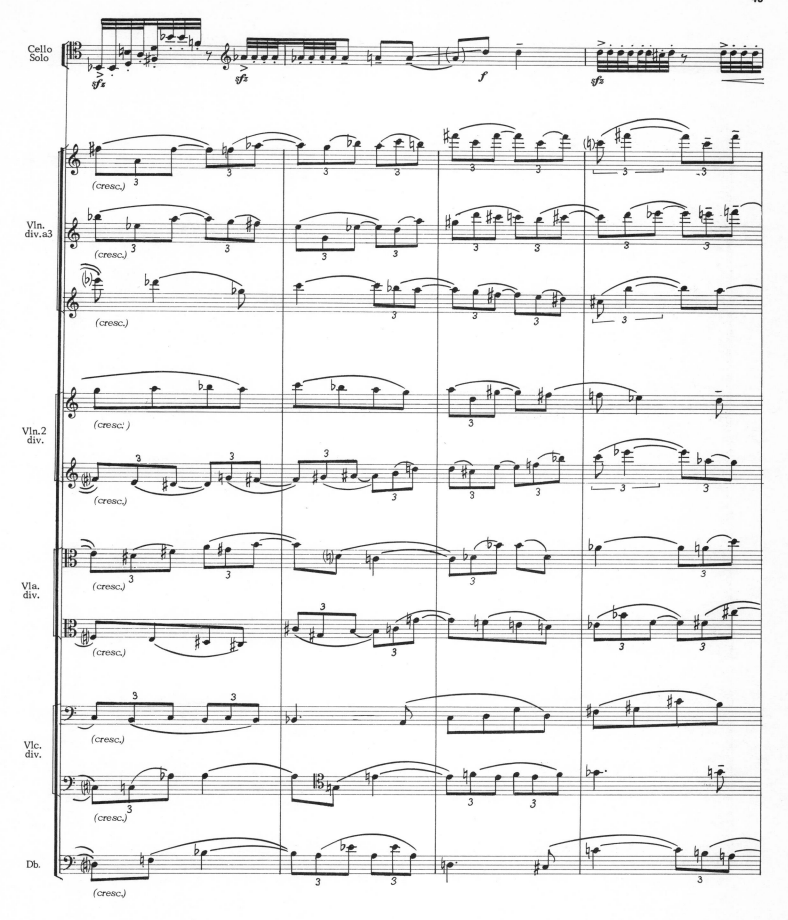

89 stringendo

string.

90 Più animato (♪= c. 144)

tornando al

Tempo principale
(♪ = 132)

58

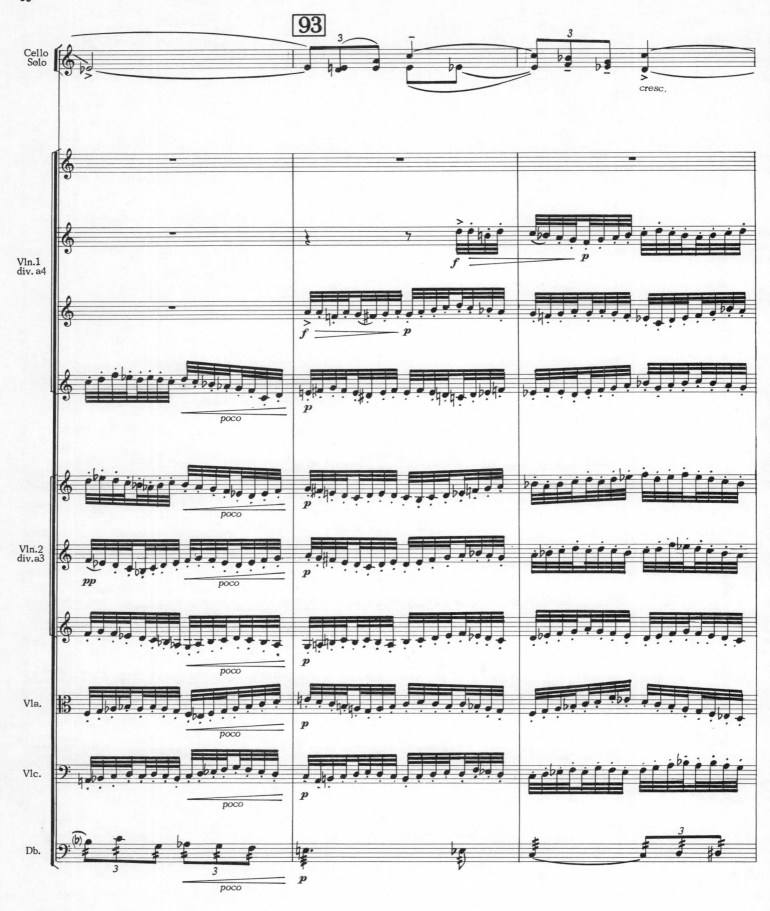

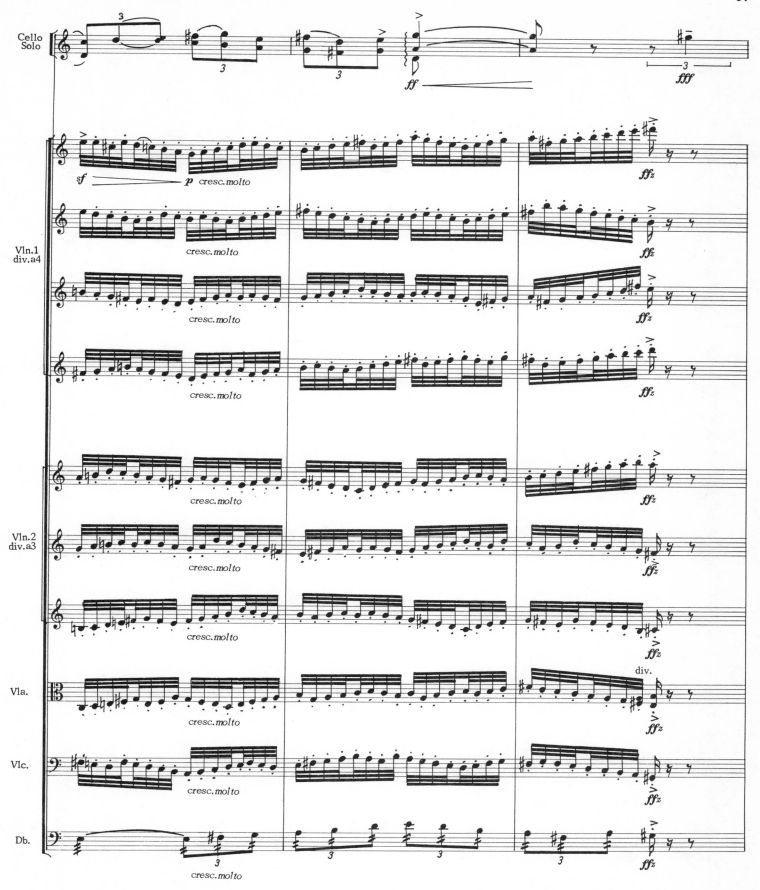

64

* For the next thirteen bars gradually reduce the number of players down to one desk per part at fig. 99 and solos three bars later.